MINDFULNESS EXERCISES
FOR DBT THERAPISTS

Copyright 2011
Edited by Karyn Hall Ph.D.

Dear Mindfulness Leader,

Very few of the following exercises are original. Most are variations or exact replicas of exercises I've learned at conferences or found in various places. I wish I could give credit to the original source for each one, but I don't know the sources. I have given credit when I know the creator, but that's only a few.

The exercises vary in terms of difficulty. Some could be dysregulating. Of course, always use your judgment about how an exercise might be received by your skills groups.

I've made an attempt to organize the exercises according to the DBT Skill they best fit. Mindfulness is a part of every skill so the division is arbitrary. Most of the exercises are directly relevant to more than one skill.

In one conference I attended Dr. Linehan cautioned group leaders to not stray from mindfulness into games or activities, that the core purpose of mindfulness is to be aware. As a group leader, being mindful of the reason for the exercises and balancing mindfulness of external and internal experiences is important. Mindfulness of internal experience can be more difficult for some group members and they may enjoy some of the more active exercises more. Group members may reinforce group leaders for using "fun" mindfulness exercises over more serious ones. So I pass this on, with the idea that each activity is about being mindful.

I hope you find these exercises helpful, either to use as they are written or to develop a variation of your own. There is really only one way to be mindful, and yet the ways to practice mindfulness are endless.

If you have mindfulness exercises you would like to share, I'd be happy to include them with or without your name, however you prefer. Please send them to me at karynhallphd@gmail.com.

Karyn Hall

Leading Mindfulness Exercises

The mindfulness skills underlie every other skill that is taught—Emotion Regulation, Distress Tolerance, and Interpersonal Effectiveness. Mindfulness is the path to wise mind. In addition, mindfulness may help group members regulate themselves for the group experience. In my experience, group members sometimes devalue the mindfulness exercise. Often they come to see it as a task to get through in order to get to what they really want to learn. Sometimes group members are very uncomfortable with mindfulness even to the point of showing up late for group, after mindfulness has been completed.

Mindless Mindfulness

The moans, eye-rolling, complaints and late arrivals "punish" therapists for taking valuable therapy time for what the client sees as a waste of time. Therapists may be concerned that clients will drop out if they don't hold their attention or they are shaped by the clients' responses.

In some groups therapists may hurry through the exercises and perhaps even minimize their importance. Or they turn mindfulness into fun exercises all the time. How easy it is to forget that mindfulness is the core skill. It is the only skill that the group leader leads a specific practice for in every group. Mindfulness is like the equipment we need for the other skills to work, like the airplane is necessary to fly, like the car is necessary to drive, like the football is necessary for the Super Bowl. If you don't know how to be mindful, you don't have the airplane or the car or the football and any attempts to drive or fly or win the Super Bowl will not work for long. You can't really tolerate distress, be effective interpersonally or regulate emotions if you can't be mindful.

Staying Mindful about Mindfulness

So what is the solution? Part of the team's job is to keep the therapist doing a good job for the client and not giving in to behaviors that the client reinforces that feel better in the moment but aren't good therapy. In addition, human beings have a limited amount of self-control. Yes, you can run out of self control (Heath and Heath 2f008). So when you've stood your ground over and over there will come a time when you don't have it in you to resist any more. Like the mother who finally, worn down by repeated pleadings, says, okay but just two cookies!"

So when therapists find themselves struggling with mindfulness exercises, we suggest they run, don't walk, to their team for support. In the long run, clients learning mindfulness is key to their improvement. That's important to therapists who work hard to help clients reach their goals and need to be effective for their own continued motivation.

So if you explain why mindfulness is important and clients come to therapy to get well, shouldn't that be enough? For some, it is, at least on most days. For others it's not. For some clients the problem may be that mindfulness makes them very uncomfortable. That could be because focusing their mind may bring about painful emotions. Or maybe they worry they aren't doing it right, after all their mind is jumping around all over the place. You may know that cleaning a wound is best for your health, but that doesn't mean you want to do it and sometimes doesn't mean you are willing to do it.

Orienting

So it's important, no matter how many groups you lead, to orient the group members to the reasons you are doing mindfulness exercises. It's like informed consent and helps the clients to use the exercises in the most productive way. You're also helping clients to be willing and to understand the importance of the exercises.

Overall commitment is part of the intake. And getting commitment to cooperate may need to be repeated. So if group leaders repeatedly have an issue with someone participating in mindfulness, then the group leaders could ask the individual therapist to assist.

Relevance and Context

There are some teaching strategies that could be helpful. First of all, mindfulness needs to be relevant and in context. Relevant means you don't use a motorcycle gang example with a group of soccer moms. And in context means you tell a brief story that makes the exercise real. This is easier said than done.

Most group leaders could come up with one or two examples that they could tie to their own lives. Here in Houston, experiences in traffic call for mindfulness on a regular basis, so many leaders have those examples. Parenting children also gives rich opportunities for mindfulness stories. But coming up with meaningful, relevant stories to use with mindfulness exercises week after week is challenging. We have to use energy. It gets easier to just do a mindfulness exercise and forget the context. That's a slippery slope into mindless mindfulness exercises. Doing mindfulness mindlessly is not helpful.

In addition, when you forget the context you've lost a huge step in how people learn. I can still remember the opening mindfulness exercise done in my intensive training because the trainer told a story about herself that fit with the exercise. I can't tell you what mindfulness exercise I led at our last team meeting because I didn't put it in context. Remembering the exercise is not the important point, but if you remember the exercise you are also more likely to remember the meaning. You're also more likely to buy in and be involved in the mindfulness exercise. That means the clients are more likely to participate fully and learn sharpen their mindfulness skill rather than go through the motions.

One answer to the problem of putting mindfulness exercises in context is to practice mindfulness yourself. Teaching mindfulness in context is almost impossible to do unless you have your own mindfulness practice.

Cindy Sanderson gave a beautiful example of putting mindfulness in context in her mindfulness exercise about an aquarium. She described going to the aquarium and seeing all different sizes, colors and shapes of fish. She then noted how our emotions can be like the fish in the aquarium.

To help you remember the importance of context, and to give you some ideas about context, I've included some examples with a few of the mindfulness exercises. These are only to give examples. The context that you use will be what you have experienced. Giving context also gives you another opportunity to model effectives use of the skills.

MINDFULNESS INSTRUCTIONS

As always, remember the basic mindfulness instructions with each exercise.

1. Get into a mindfulness position.
2. Give the name of the practice exercise.
3. Give context, usually by telling a personal story.
4. Explain the practice.
5. Remind the participants to gently bring their mind back if and when it wanders.
6. Ask if there are any questions.
7. Ring the bell three times.
8. Participate.
9. Ring the bell one time.
10. Give opportunity to describe experience.

Distress Tolerance

Scrambled Count

Context: I have never enjoyed numbers. Mention multiplication and I am immediately daydreaming about going to the beach. My eyes glaze over if your conversation contains numbers that don't refer to someone's age. I become most unmindful. I've realized that I associate numbers with algebra and geometry, classes that were hard for me in school. I'm judging numbers because of something that happened in my past. So I thought I could be mindful of numbers in a fun way, help my brain see the way numbers really are instead of reacting based on long ago experiences. So this mindfulness

Primary Mindfulness Component: Participate

Primary related skill: Distress Tolerance

Materials: none

Directions. Give the group a set of numbers in order with one or two numbers more than the number of group members. If you have six group members, you could give the numbers one through seven, or twenty-one through twenty-eight.

The first person says a number. The second person says a number but doesn't repeat the number already said. This continues until you are back to the first person. The second time around the members cannot repeat the number they said in the previous round.

If someone repeats on purpose a number someone else said in that round, then the round starts over and that person gets to start. If they are "caught" by the other members then the round starts over and they are the last person.

After doing this a few times, each member talks about his or her experience. Some members will feel pressure and stress. It can be interesting to point out how the mind creates anxiety when there is no need for flight or fight, no consequence in reality.

Imagery, Favorite Place

Context: Yesterday was one of those days when everything goes wrong. I woke up late because I forgot to set my alarm. I got out of bed and didn't have any coffee. The dress I wanted to wear was in the laundry and the electricity went out before I finished blow-drying my hair. I get to my car and I realize I have to stop at the gas station to get gas, and I'm already late for work. So I arrive at work irritable and ready to snap at my co-workers though they have nothing to do with any of these events.

I could go through my day cranky and mean, and probably making it worse each hour. But I remembered a mindfulness exercise that I love because I have a very relaxing favorite place. So today we're going to do a mindfulness exercise about being mindful of the positive.

Directions: Get in an awake position. Lower your eyes. Now picture yourself at your favorite place. If you don't have a favorite place, create one. Picture what you are wearing. See the colors of your clothes. How does the material feel next to your skin? Feel the air on your body. What type of floor or ground do you feel under your feet? What do you see when you look around you? What shapes, what colors? What do you smell? Are you moving? What is that movement like? How do you feel being in this place?

Put the Glass Down

Directions: Read the following story. After you have read the story, allow some quiet time for mindfulness about the story. Then check with the members about how mindful they were able to be.

A professor was giving a lecture to his students on stress management. He raised a glass of water and asked the audience, "How heavy do you think this glass of water is?"   The students' answers ranged fro 20g to 500 gm. "It does not matter on the absolute weight. It depends on how long you hold it. If I hold it for a minute it is okay. If I hold it for an hour, I will have an ache in my right arm. If I hold it for a day, you will have to call an ambulance. It is the exact same weight, but the longer I hold it, the heavier it becomes. If we carry our burdens all the time, sooner or later, we will not be able to carry on as the burden becomes increasingly heavier. What you have to do is put the glass down, rest for while before holding it up again. We have to put down the burden periodically so that we can be refreshed and are able to carry on.

Author
Unknown

Pinwheels

Supplies: A pinwheel for each member of the group

Primary Skill: Observe the breath

Directions: Focus on the breath. Focus on the breath all the way in. Now focus on the breath all the way out. Let your breath turn the pinwheel. Focus on the breath turning the pinwheel slowly or faster.

A Box of Chocolates

Skill Targeted: Willingness, Radical Acceptance

Supplies: A box of chocolate candy with different fillings and a guide to the fillings (usually on the lid of the box)

Optional: Tissues for choosing the chocolate.

Directions: "I am going to pass around a box of chocolates. Please select one."

After the group has made their selections, say "Now I want you to give your chocolate to the person on your right." After they have passed their chocolate, say "Be mindful of your internal reaction."

Stones
Jon Kabat- Zinn

Primary Skill: Radical Acceptance

Materials: Stones, water and cups for each member, chimes

Directions: Have members choose a stone and pass out cups. Ask them to put a small amount of water in each cup.

Say: Have you ever floated on a tube or a boat down a shallow river and noticed the beautiful rocks as you pass? They look so beautiful when the sun shines through the water and reflects the colors. As I float by I don't want the experience to end. It is so peaceful. I also see rocks that I don't want to leave. But then there are more rocks further down. Sometimes I think that is the way life is too, that you don't want to leave some times in your life that are good and yet there are different experiences to come if we let them and are patient.

When you hear the chimes, please observe your rock. When you hear the chimes again, put your rock in water and observe it again. When the chimes ring three times, the exercise is over.

Self Soothing Sharing

Supplies: Either bring or have a group member bring in an object they use for one of the senses. You could do this multiple times covering all the senses. Some ideas are

Hearing: music, forest sounds, silence, voice of a favorite person

Taste: Lemons, sugar, chocolate, mint

Seeing: Art, photos of nature, pictures of favorite people, colors, books, pictures of a pet

Smell: candles with different smells, cologne, soaps, herbs,

Touch: soft material, smooth stones, rubbing your shoulders, rubbing a pen back and forth on your palms, hugging yourself

The group member or group leader shares the object and the group members is asked to be mindful of the object shared.

Not Knowing

Materials: A medium size box or bag

Primary Skill: Observe, Mindful of Current Emotion

Directions: As you can see there is a box in front of me on the table. There is something in this box, but you don't know what it is. Focus on what it is like to not know. Observe how your mind reacts to not knowing.

After 30 seconds you might want to give a hint. Or suggest they silently guess what is in the box and notice how it feels to guess.

After discussing not knowing and guessing you might end the exercise. Someone will want to know what was in the box. You can then discuss what it is like to not find out something that you expected to learn. You can either stop with that, ask them to sit and observe their feelings, or reveal what is in the box. What is inside doesn't matter, but it might be interesting for it to be fruit or a snack of some sort.

Observe the Breath
(Julia P. Layman, MSW)

Primary Skill: Observe

Materials: Drinking straws, one for each group member

Directions: Using the straw, breath all the way in and all the way out.

Music
(From participants in DBT Training, May 18, 2004)

Primary Skill: Self Soothe

Materials: Play different types of music. As you play each piece ask group members to write the emotions created by each piece. Be mindful of which ones are soothing to each person.

Scent
Materials: Cotton balls and different scents, like essential oils

Directions: Put different smells on the cotton balls and smell them. Be mindful of your response to each scent. Note which smells are soothing to you.

Mindfulness of the Breath Stress Release

Primary Skill: Self Soothing

Directions: With an inhale, think of all the things in your life that are giving you stress/worry/anxiety. Breathe in all that stress in a count of five, then quickly blow out the entire breath in a count of two.

Emotion Regulation

Grandfather Tells

Directions: Read the following story and ask the group to be mindful.

An old Grandfather said to his grandson, who came to him with anger at a friend who had done him an injustice, "Let me tell you a story. I too at times have felt a great hate for those that have taken so much with no sorrow for what they do.

But hate wears you down and does not hurt your enemy. It is like taking poison and wishing your enemy would die. I have struggled with these feelings many times." He continued, "It is as if there are two wolves inside me. One is good and does no harm. He lives in harmony with all around him and does not take offense when no offense was intended. He will only fight when it is right to do so an in the right way.

But the other wolf, ah! He is full of anger. The littlest thing will set him into a fit of temper. He fights everyone all the time for no reason. He cannot think because his anger and hate are so great. It is helpless anger for his anger will change nothing. Sometimes it is hard to live with these two wolves inside me for both of them try to dominate my spirit.

The boy looked intently into his Grandfather's eyes and asked, "Which one wins, Grandfather?" The Grandfather smiled and quietly said, "The one I feed."

Anger

Supplies: A recording of voices shouting in anger

Directions: In real life one of the times it can most help to be mindful is when others are dysregulated. Today we are going to practice with a recording of angry voices. As you listen be mindful of your own reactions and use your skills to self soothe.

Play the recording for a minute.

Discuss how mindful they were and how the were able to soothe themselves.

Collecting Pleasant Memories

Goal: Increase awareness of positive events

Have group members list positive events that can occur on a regular basis. Examples include: Someone smiles at you, holds door open, see a beautiful sunset, have food that you like, spend time with a friend, do an activity you enjoy, someone says thank you, learn something new, watch a good movie, read a good book.

Directions to group: The mind tends to notice and hold on to events and emotions that occur that are not pleasant. At one time that might have helped survival, such as remembering plants that made you sick. Today holding on to uncomfortable feelings is often hurtful rather than helpful and to hold on to the unpleasant while giving little attention to the pleasant means your emotional bank account is always in the red.

Beginning to focus on pleasant events may be uncomfortable because you are not used to doing it. You may discount many pleasant events as silly or unimportant because your fears and irrational thoughts tell you only the unpleasant count or matter because they hurt so much. Strive for willingness, as noticing pleasant feelings and sensations is critical.

For the next few minutes, focus on a small pleasant experience you have had. It might be that someone smiled at you when you needed that acceptance, someone held the door open for you, you noticed a beautiful sunset, the taste of your favorite food, time with a friend, participating in an activity you enjoy, watching a good movie, reading a good book, petting a dog or cat. For some it could be the feel of clean sheets or going to bed when you are really tired.

Focus on those good feelings for a few moments. Notice any discomfort you may have, any way your mind attempts to discount those feelings and let it go, gently bring your mind back to the pleasant feeling.

Drawing
Jill Tiedemann, LPCC

Primary Skill: Observe

Materials: Copies of a simple pencil drawing for each group member, pencil and paper for each group member

Directions: Give the drawing to the group members and ask them to observe it mindfully. After a minute or so, ask them to put the drawing away and replicate it.

Internal Tour and Check In

Goal: To notice emotions, connect emotions to physical sensations, to use skills to manage emotions and learn not to act on emotions

Directions to Group: Take a breath. Slowly release. Take another breath. Slowly release. Focus for a moment on your feelings. Notice if there is any sadness. Just notice. Notice if there is any shame. Just notice. Notice if there is any anger. Just notice. Notice if there is any joy. Just notice. Notice if there is any anxiety. Just notice.

Now notice your thoughts. Are they focused on one situation? Are they changing rapidly or slowly? Just notice.

Now notice your body. Any pain? Any soreness? Are your muscles relaxed or tense?
Just notice.

Now come back into this room. Notice your reaction to this internal tour.

Were you mindful?

Blue Dot

Materials: Blue Dot drawn on board or a large blue dot cut from construction paper

Small blue dot stickers from office supply store

Directions: Ask the group members to be mindful of the blue dot. As they focus on the blue dot to also self soothe. Be in the moment. Slow the breath. Let go of all thoughts except the blue dot. Let time pass in quiet.

Discuss the mindfulness. Then hand out the blue dot stickers. Ask the group members to put the dots on different belongings or around the area where they live and where they work and their car. Every time they see a blue dot to practice mindfulness. You might want to put some blue dots in the group room and the therapy offices.

Peacock Feather
Jill Tiedemann, LPCC

Primary Skill: One mindfully

Materials: Long peacock feathers for each member

Directions: Give each member a feather. Ask them to observe their feather. Now ask them to balance their feather on their hand, being mindful only of their own feather

Awareness of Brain Filling in Meaning

Materials: Hand out the following paragraph on a piece of paper. Ask the group to read it to themselves. After they have read the paragraph ask them to be mindful of how it is written and how the brain makes meaning out of the words.

The Paomnnehal Pwer of the Hmuan Mnid

Acccdrnig to a rscheearch at Cmabrigde Uivervtisy, it deosn't mttaer in what order the ltteers in a word are, the olny iprmoatnt thing is that the frist and lsat ltteer be in the rghit pclae. The rset can be a taotl mses and you can still raed it wouthit porbelm. This is becusae the human mind deos not raed ervey teter by istlef, but the word as a wlohe.

Guest House

Primary Skill: Awareness of current emotion

Directions: Read the following poem and ask the group to listen mindfully.

The Guest House

This being human is a guest house.
Every morning a new arrival.

A joy, a depression, a meanness,
some momentary awareness comes
as an unexpected visitor.

Welcome and entertain them all!
Even if they're a crowd of sorrows,
who violently sweep your house
empty of its furniture,
still, treat each guest honorably.
He may be clearing you out
for some new delight.

The dark thought, the shame, the malice,
meet them at the door laughing,
and invite them in.

Be grateful for whoever comes,
because each has been sent
as a guide from beyond.

Rumi

Mindfulness

Snowflakes
Juliet Nelson

Primary Skill: Nonjudgmentally

Materials: Scissors and paper for each group member

Directions: Fold the paper and cut out designs

Rice in Sand

Materials: Baggies filled with sand and 4 to 5 grains of rice

Directions: Pass out one baggie to each group member. Ask the group to feel the sandbag in their hands. Then ask the group members to find the grains of rice in their baggie without dumping the sand out.

Share how mindful each group member was able to be and how they managed the feelings they had about finding the grains of rice.

Trip to the Zoo

Focus on being present

The first member of the group takes the letter A and says I went to the zoo and I saw an A (e.g., antelope, aardvark, ape), listing one animal. The next member repeats what the first member said and adds an animal that start with a b.

Eyewitness

Primary Skill: Observe and Describe

Ask one member to leave the room. While he or she is out of the room, she or he is to change something about their appearance. When they return to the group room, the members are asked what they changed.

Rhythm Game
(From participants in DBT Training, May 18, 2004)

Primary Skill: One Mindfully

Directions: Go around in a circle. Start with a rhythm sound/gesture. Each person repeats the previous one(s) and adds one. If someone misses, they step back and become a distractor.

Buzz
(From participants in DBT Training, May 18, 2004)

Primary Skill: One Mindfully

Directions: Choose a number, such as 3 and use derivations of 3 (3,6,9,12,15) as the buzzword instead of saying actual number. Go around the circle. Start with 1, 2, and the next person says "Buzz." 4, 5, "Buzz" and so on. If someone miscounts or buzzes at the wrong time, that person steps out and becomes a distractor.

Snap, Crackle, and Pop
(From participants in DBT Training, May 18, 2004)

Primary Skill: Participate

Directions: Snap: Cross your arm over chest either left or right
                 Crackle: Cross arm over head either left or right
                 Pop: Point to someone in circle in any direction

Person pointed at is "it" next. Keep sequence going by speaking and gesturing. Go in order Snap (person pointed to is next), Crackle (person pointed to is next) Pop (person pointed to is next). If someone misspeaks or misgestures, have the individual step outside the circle and become a distractor.

Name Game
(From participants in DBT Training, May 18, 2004)

Directions: Go around in a circle. Say the name of a famous person, such as Abe Lincoln. The next person says a name that starts with the first letter of the previous last name, such as Lesley Horne. If both the first and last names start with the same letter, such as Sharon Stone, then you reverse direction in the circle.

Lemons

Primary Skill: Observe

Supplies: Enough lemons or oranges or apples for each group member to have one
A bowl that allows the fruit to be easily observed

Directions: Ask each group member to take a lemon. Ask the group to be mindful of the lemon they chose. Then ask them to return their lemon to the bowl. When all lemons have been returned to the bowl, mix them up. Then ask each member to find the lemon they had.

This exercise can also be done with coins.

Foot in Air
(Juliet Nelson)

Primary Skill: Nonjudgmentally

Directions: While sitting, lift your right foot off the floor and make clockwise circles. Now, while doing this, draw the number 6 in the air with your right hand.

Note: The foot will typically change directions.

Listen

Primary Skill: Observe
Directions: Listen and be mindful of all the sounds that you hear.

Observe and Describe
(Julia P. Layman, MSW)

Directions: Look around you carefully. Observe the room you are in. Truly look at the room carefully. (Allow about two minutes.) Now describe what you saw.

Group Drawing

Supplies: Colored pencils or crayons for each member of the group or enough to share a   A piece of white paper for each member of the group

Directions to the Group: Please draw whatever you wish on the paper you have. Be mindful of your thoughts and emotions as you draw. Wait about 1 minute. Then ask the group members to pass the paper to the person on their right. Wait another minute and the ask them to pass to the right again. Continue until each paper has returned to its original owner. If you have a very small group you may wish to lengthen the time before the paper is passed or pass multiple times.

Ask about their ability to be mindful and what they noticed about themselves.

Mindful Walking

Directions: For mindfulness today we are going to do mindful walking. What I want you to do is be aware of each step, be aware as each part of your foot touches the floor, and be aware of your leg as it moves. Focus your attention on the experiences of walking. If you begin to think, gently bring your mind back to walking and your body's movements as you walk.

The leader begins walking with the group members to follow.

Discussion of how mindful each person was.

Create a Dance

Primary Skill: Participate

Supplies: Music

Directions: Ask group members to stand. Then ask each group member to create a dance move and the rest of the group will do the dance move with the member who created it.

Taste

(I believe this one is from Jon Kabat-Zinn)

Primary Skill: Observe

Materials: Raisin or strawberry or piece of chocolate

Directions: Pause between the statements. Examine the food that you have. Notice the way it feels. Be mindful of the indentations, the marks, and the surface of it. Then, without biting it, place the food in your mouth. Hold it there and explore it. Notice the feel of it. Now slowly bite into it. Hold it in the front of your tongue. Move it to the side of your tongue. Move it to the back of your tongue. Be mindful of the taste; be mindful of how it feels in your mouth. Now slowly chew, being aware of each spurt of flavor. Swallow when you are ready.

Sound Toss

Primary Skill: Participate

Directions: One person in the group makes a sound, and then points to another group member. That group member repeats the sound, makes a new sound, and points to another group member. Continue for a minute or so, depending on group size.

Table Slap

Primary Skill: Participate

Directions: Put both hands on the table. When it is your turn you can either slap the table or pound lightly with your fist. If you use your fist, you reverse the order. If you slap with the hand that goes first then use your fist with your second hand, the order reverses and you must either slap or pound with your other hand. If you pound your fist twice, it skips the next turn (either the first hand of the next person or your other hand). If you go out of turn, you take that hand out of the exercise.

Rain
(From participants in DBT Training, May 18, 2004)

Directions: Pick a leader and divide everyone else into groups. Everyone follows the directions of the leader and otherwise is silent. The actions/sounds in order are:

1. Rub hands together
2. Snap fingers
3. Rap on table (or stamp feet)
4. Snap fingers
5. Rub hands together

The leader goes from group to group, rubbing hands together and adding each group one at a time until all are doing the same action/noise. The leader continues going around the room, switching the groups one at a time to the second action until all the groups have switched to that sound, then continue around the room, switching one group at a time to the third sound.

Finger painting

Primary Skill: Participate

Materials: Finger paints and paper

Directions: Be mindful of your experience as you finger paint

Concentration

Primary Skill: Observe

Supplies: On index cards write the names of skills. Write the same skill on two index cards. You may wish to include a Wild Card that will match any card. Lay the index cards on the table in front of the group.

Directions: Ask each group member to be mindful of their judgments. Each group member turns over two cards, one at a time, attempting to get a match. If she gets a match she can try again until she fails to get a match. When she fails to get a match it is the next player's turn.

Points of View

Primary Skill: Observe and Describe

Supplies: Music played with different instruments. Jazz is a good option.

Directions: Play a piece of the music and ask the group to focus on one instrument such as the piano. Then play it again and ask them to be mindful on a different instrument such as the saxophone.

Discuss how their ability to be mindful and how their experience changed.

Mindful Ball Toss

Primary Skill Addressed: One Mindfully

Supplies: Two soft balls

Directions: Group members stand. Two balls are tossed at the same time. The two people with the balls call the name of another group member at the same time they toss the ball to that person.

Passing the Ball
(Jennifer Eaton, MS, LMHC)

Primary Skill: One mindfully

Materials: Small, soft balls or tennis balls

Directions: Two balls are passed back and forth across the group, down the line until it has passed between each member. Start the first ball and then when the first ball makes two passes, start the second ball. Your can a third and fourth ball depending on group size. If the ball is dropped, start over. If the table is too wide, have group members stand in two lines facing each other.

Mindful Music

Primary Skill: Structure

Materials: Toy instruments, such as xylophones for each group member

Directions: Let each person sound a note and then add all the notes together (chaos). Then have each person play their note in order, going around the room (order).
Ode to Joy has 7 notes and could be used.

Mindful Ball Scramble

Materials: Small, soft balls easily held in the hand, one for each member

Directions: Start with half the group having balls. They are to mindfully and randomly roll the balls to other group members, being mindful of catching the balls that come to them and rolling to others without hitting other balls. They cannot hold onto the balls. Ask the group to be mindful of how they react to the balls coming to them and the rolling of the balls After 30 seconds add more balls, two at a time.

Mindful Balloons Toss

Primary Skill Addressed: Participate

Supplies: Balloons, already blown up and tied

Directions: Have group members stand. Give three or four group members a balloon. They are to bat the balloon in the air and keep them from touching the table or the floor. After a minute or so, add additional balloons.

Beads

Primary Skill: Observe

Materials: A large bowl of beads or buttons or multicolored stones

Directions: Pass the bowl around the room. Each member is to mindfully choose one stone/bead/button. Be mindful of your button/bead/stone/

Describe your object to the group. Keep the button as a reminder to be mindful.

Coloring

Primary Skill: Observe, participate

Materials: A page from a coloring book for each member, or a page that can be colored and crayons or colored pencils for each member

Directions: Color the picture with your nondominant hand.

Upper Lip
(Marsha Linehan, Ph.D.)

Primary Skill: Observe

Directions: Rub your upper lip. Notice how long you feel a sensation.

Breathing Patience
(Bonnie Atkins, LICSW)

Directions: Read the following quotation:

Do you have the patience to wait
Til your mud settles and the water is clear?
Can you remain unmoving
Til the right action arises by itself?
Lao Tzu

Then inhale and exhale with the following phrases said out loud or to yourself:

Breathing in: Waiting patiently
Breathing out: My mind settles

Breathing in: Remaining still
Breathing out: Wise mind arises

Yarn
(Bonnie Atkins LICSW)

Primary Skill: One Mindfully

Materials: A small ball of yarn

Directions: Pass the yarn from group member to group member (in order) until the yarn is unwound. Then wind it up again by passing it back

Mandala
Maine Medical Center Adolescent DBT

Primary Skill: Observe

Materials: Give each member a sheet of paper with a large circle on it and crayons or colored pencils

Directions: Color how you feel inside the circle

Drawing

Primary Skills: Nonjudgmentally, participate, observe, describe

Materials: Pencil and paper for every group member, tape
Directions: Have members tape the paper to the table in front of them, just enough so it stays in place. "Put your dominant hand on the table. Now looking only at your dominant hand, draw that hand with your nondominant hand.

Members then describe their internal experience.

Flashlight
(Bonnie Atkins, LICSW)

Primary Skill: Observe

Materials: Flashlight, dark room

Directions: In a dark room, shine the flashlight on one object. Ask the group to focus their attention on the one object.

Singing in Rounds

Primary Skill: Participate, One Mindfully

Directions: Divide the group into halves. The first group starts singing Row, Row Row Your Boat. The second group starts singing when the first group gets to the end of the first phrase. You can divide the group into thirds as well.

Row, row, row your boat
Gently down the stream
Merrily, merrily, merrily, merrily
Life is but a dream.

Other songs can be done this way too, such as The Lion Sleeps Tonight

Singing with Hand Movements

Primary Skill: Participate

Directions: Sing a song like "Take me out to the Ballgame" and add hand motions

Take me out to the ball game (Both hands point to self)
Take me out with the crowd (Both hands sweep around)
Buy me some peanuts and Cracker Jack (Point to the right)
I don't care if I never get back, (Shake head)
Let me root, root, root for the home team, (hands in fists, shaking in rhythm)
If they don't win it's a shame. (Cover face)
For it's one, two, three strikes, you're out, (One finger two fingers, three fingers)
At the old ball game. (Hands up)

Saying Numbers or Alphabet
(Bonnie Atkins, LICSW)

Primary Skill: One Mindfully

Directions: One person starts with A or 1. The others in the room follow (not in order) with the next number or letter. If tow people speak at the same time, start over.

What You Think of Me (Reading)
(Dennis Merritt Jones, DD)

Primary Skill: Nonjudgmental

A student went to his master teacher and asked to be taught the key to true inner peace and freedom from emotional suffering.

The master said to him, "Go to the cemetery and curse the person that lay in each grave. Tell them that they are stupid and their mother is ugly too. After you have done that then go back again the next day and bless and praise each person in every grave, telling them how wonderful they are…tell them that the world worships the to this day…even go so far as to light incense and candles for each one, calling them saints. When you have done this, come back to me.

The student dutifully did as instructed. Upon returning the master asked the student, "Well, what did they have to say about your opinions?"

Astounded, the student replied, "How could they respond to me at all? They were all dead and could not hear a word I said, negative or positive."

The master replied, "When you too do not hear what others have to say about you, negative or positive, you will know true inner peace and freedom from suffering

Simon Says

Primary Skill: One Mindfully

Directions: One group member is Simon. Simon gives easy directions to the group. The group members are to do what he says only if he says Simon Says. For example: If the leader says "life your right foot" the group should not follow the direction. If he says, "Simon says lift your left foot" then the group members should do the command. If any member misses then he is out and can be a distractor or wait for the others to finis

Watching Thoughts
(By Marsha Linehan. She used this one at a conference, but I don't remember the date. I have not listed the same words she used because I don't remember them.)

Primary Skill: Observe and Describe

Directions: I am going to say some words. As I say the words I want you to be mindful of how the words come into your mind, what your experience is as I say these words.

Stampede	Mountain	Serendipitous	Birthday
Love	Yellow		
Chocolate	Surprise	Rocking Chair	Tree
Pillow	Beautiful		

Discussion: Encourage discussion of their internal experience. If they do not offer many ideas, ask questions such as the following:

Did the thoughts come in the center or from the side?

Did you see images?
Did you see colors?

Mindful of the Senses
(Suzaane Robinson, LCSW)

Primary Skill: Observe

Directions: Take a deep breath at your own comfort level. Release.
Another deep breath. Release.

Be mindful of five sounds.

Be mindful of five smells.

Be mindful of five things you can taste right now.

Be mindful of five things you can see right now.

Be mindful of five things you can touch right now.

Interpersonal Effectiveness

Two Truths and a Lie

Primary Skill: Nonverbal communication

Directions: Each person tells two truths and a lie about himself. Others try to figure out which is the lie. Emphasize body language.

Telephone

Primary Skill: Mindful Listening

Directions: Whisper a message or a phrase to the person next to you. That person is to listen mindfully and whisper the same message to the next person. Each person whispers to the next until the message is given to the last person. That person says what she heard.

Empathy

Supplies: A brief story. A fable from *Aesop's Fables. Wisdom Tales From Around the World* or a U-tube video or a clip from a movie

Directions: Name a character and ask them to be mindful of how that character feels. Then read the story or play the video. Then name a different character. Ask them to be mindful of that character and how he feels. Then reread the story or replay the video.

Discuss how the story was different from each viewpoint and the experience of being mindful of different characters.

Mindful Conversation
Beverly Bontrager, LCSW

You can do this with the whole group or divide into dyads. Focus on mindful listening and mindfully asking questions. Remind the group what mindful listening and mindful body language is. Then give the following instruction:

Remember when you are speaking to pause and give the listener(s) an opportunity to comment or ask a question. See if you can be aware of the response you are getting from the listener. Be mindful of "we" not "me" or "you." When you are listening, listen fully, focus on the person, not on what you want to say. If your mind wanders, gently bring it back. You are also being mindful of "we" not "me" or "you."

For mindful conversation, we are going to talk about television shows. Each person will talk about their favorite television show. When I ring the bell, the person who was speaking becomes the listener and the listener becomes the speaker. (Or the person to the right becomes the next speaker.)

Body Language

Supplies: Paper and pencil for each group member

Directions: On a large piece of paper or on a white board write a list of emotions: fear, anger, surprise, joy, shame, scorn, frustration

Make a list of the same emotions in a different order that you do not share with the group members.

"I am going to make a series of facial expressions that represent the emotions I've listed on the board. Here's the first Give a facial expression. Continue for each emotion on your list, letting the group know when you are changing your expression. Ask the group members to write the name of each emotion you portray.

What were they mindful about for each expression?

Connections with Others

Directions: Pause between each statement. Ask each group member to hand an object that they own to the member on their right. Each member is to be mindful of the object and the connection to the person who handed it to them. Mindfully return the object.

Ungame

Primary Skill: Observing nonverbal communication, recognizing emotions in nonverbal

Materials: Deck of Ungame Cards

Directions: Pass the deck of cards with emotions to be depicted and then pass the cards with the statement to be made. Each group member is to say the statement while at the same time using body language and tone to show the emotion that likely doesn't match the statement. Group members are to guess the emotion being expressed.

Loving Kindness

Directions: (Pause between suggestions) Get in a comfortable awake position. Relax your muscles. Focus on your breath. Now be mindful of a simple, positive experience you have had with someone else. Be mindful of the details of that experience. Be aware of the feelings that experience creates or brings about. Take in those feelings, be mindful of them. Now send those feelings to someone you love. Now send them to a pet or a friend or someone you have met. You may send the feelings to a group, to your family, to the whole country, to the whole world. Now send them to the person on your right. Be aware of the person on your left sending loving kindness to you.

Connected

Directions: (Pause between each statement.) Get in a comfortable, awake position. Focus on your breath coming in. Focus on your breath going out.

Be aware of how your breath in takes from the same air as the rest of the people in the room. Be aware of how you breathe out and others breath in the same air you just breathed out. Be aware of the connectedness of all people sharing the same air. Be aware of your chair. Feel the connection between the chair and your body. Notice how the chair feels. Be aware of the seat of the chair being connected to the legs of the chair. Be aware of your body on the seat of the chair that is connected to the legs of the chair. Be aware of the legs of the chair on the floor of the room. And the legs of your chair on the same floor as the legs of the chair of the person next to you. Of all the people in the room. Feel the connectedness of everyone connected to the same floor. And the floor of the building is connected to the walls that are connected to the ground. We are all connected to the ground and to each other. And to the rest of the people in the world.

Priorities and Demands

Materials: Golf balls, pebbles, mayonnaise jar, sand two cups of coffee. Or this can be done as a reading

Directions: After group starts, fill the mayonnaise jar with golf balls. Ask if the jar is full. Then take the bag of pebbles and pour into the jar. Ask if the jar is full. Then take a box of sand out of a bag or from a hidden place and pour sand in the jar. Ask if the jar is full. Then take two cups of coffee from a hidden place and pour those into the jar.

READING
The Mayonnaise Jar and Coffee

When things in your life seem almost too much to handle, when 24 hours in a day are not enough, remember the mayonnaise jar and the coffee.

A professor stood before his philosophy class and had some items in front of him. When the class began, he picked up a very large and empty mayonnaise jar and proceeded to fill it with golf balls. He then asked if the jar was full. They said it was. The professor next picked up a box of pebbles and poured them into the jar. Then he asked if the jar was full. Then he took a bag of sand and poured that into the jar. Of course the sand filled up everything else. He asked once more if the jar was full. The students responded yes. The professor then produced two cups of coffee from under the table and poured the entire contents into the jar, effectively filling the empty space between the sand. The students laughed.

"Now, the professor said, "I want you to think about this jar representing your life. The golf balls are the important things, your friends, children, family, favorite passions, things that if everything else was lost and only they remained your life would still be full. The pebbles are the other things that matter like enough food to eat, clothes to wear. The sand is everything else—the small stuff.

If you put the sand into the jar first there is no room for the pebbles or the golf balls. The same goes for life. If you spend all your time and energy on the small stuff, you will never have room for the things that are important to you.

Pay attention to the things that are critical to you. Oh and the coffee? It just goes to show you that no matter how full your life is you always have room for a couple of cups of coffee with a friend.

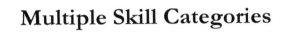

Multiple Skill Categories

Skill Generalization/Improving Recall

Recalling Skills Bingo
Beverly Bontrager, MSW, DBT Center Houston

Primary Skill: Recall of all skills

Materials: Pencil, paper, list of categories such as Skills, Relationships, Tolerance, Emotions, Wants, Shoulds, Priorities, Mindfulness. Numbers on small pieces of paper folded in a container

Directions: Have the group members draw the numbers from the container to see who chooses the letter. You can have any number be the "winner." The person who gets the winning number chooses a letter. Then the group writes all the words they can think of that go in the categories that start with that letter.

Dialectical Thinking

Red and Yellow
Materials: Small baggie with ketchup and mustard, separated

Directions: Slowly mix the two. Be mindful of the dialectic

Six Sticks

Materials: sticks, like matchsticks, three for each group member

Ask the group members to arrange the sticks so they have six instead of three.

Two solutions are to make the number 6 and to make the Roman numeral 6.

Fairy Tales

Have group members be mindful of fairy tale or cartoon villains or characters other than the main protagonist, such as the Big Bad Wolf, the Evil Queen in Snow White, Captain Hook, Wiley Coyote, Queen of Hearts (Alice in Wonderland), Scar (The Lion King), Prince John (Robin Hood), Cruella DeVille (101 Dalmatians), Shere Kahn (The Jungle Book), and Maleficent (Sleeping Beauty). Ask them to consider the story from that character's point of view.

DBT Charades

Primary Skill: Distress Tolerance and Mindfulness (participate)

Put names of DBT skills on slips of paper and have each group member draw a slip of paper. Each member then acts out the name of the skill without using words.

Skills to list:
Wise Mind
Self soothe, vision
Self soothe, touch
Radical Acceptance
Self soothe, smell
Self soothe, hearing
Distract, activities
Distract, contribution
Distract, comparisons
Distract, opposite emotions
Distract, pushing away
Distract, thoughts
Self soothe, sensations

The member who guesses the skill then gives an example of the skill. You may have each member give an example of the skill as well.

Dialectical Jeopardy

Joquetta Hutchens

Primary Skill: Participate

Materials: Flip chart or board, markers, questions prepared for each category and double jeopardy questions as well, noise makers for each person

Directions: At the top write DIALECTICAL JEOPARDY. Then draw a grid underneath with three columns and four or five rows. At the top of each column write the name of the category, such as emotion regulation, distress tolerance, mindfulness, or miscellaneous.

Put 100 on each square of the first row, put 200 on each square in the second row. Then a group member (perhaps the newest?) picks a question. If she can't answer the question, encourage her to use her notes or her book. You can have people use noise makers of some sort or raise their hand to answer the question. A very new member could be score keeper.

Sample Questions

Mindfulness
Name the three mindfulness what skills
Name the three mindfulness how skills
Give an example of effectiveness
Define mindfulness

Miscellaneous
Give an example of a dialectic
Describe how to functionally validate someone whose toe you just stepped on
Describe how to self validate when you have lost a game
What are the four possible actions to take in any situation?

Emotion Regulation
Describe a situation in which you might use Opposite Action
Describe wants versus demands
How do you build mastery?

Interpersonal Effectiveness
What does DEAR MAN stand for?
What does GIVE stand for?
When do you use GIVE?
What does FAST stand for? When do you use FAST?
What are the three primary goals of every interaction?

Distress Tolerance
What does IMPROVE stand for?
Give an example of how to self-soothe using senses
How do you turn the mind?
Describe when to use half smile
Give an example of radical acceptance
How do you do pros and cons?

DBT Wheel of Fortune
(Joquetta Hutchens)

Primary Skill: Participate

Materials: Flip Chart of Paper or board, markers

Directions: Draw a circle on the top half of your flip chart, dividing it into six or eight pie pieces. The number depends on how long you want to guess letters.

On the bottom half of the flip chart, put blanks corresponding to the letters of a DBT word or phrase

Go around the group letting members and co-therapists guess letters to the word/phrase. They can guess any letter they want.

If the guesser guesses a letter correctly, they get to guess again. If they wish, they can guess the phrase or word.

If they guess a letter that's not in the word/phrase, place that letter in the pie circle. If the pie circle gets full before anyone guesses the word/phrase, then reveal the word/phrase and move to the next puzzle.

When someone guesses the word/phrase, they then tell what they know about it and its being part of DBT.

The one guessing the word/phrase gets to lead the next puzzle.

Picture Puzzles

Goal: Generalization of skills

Level: Advanced

Materials: Pictures of people, animals, actions, and objects from magazines. Choose pictures that relate to healthy activities, unhealthy activities, people who look unhappy, people who look happy. You might want to include pictures of people exercising, talking with others, and pictures of healthy food. Pictures of traffic signs such as Yield and Stop and Slow usually work well. Think of the skills when you choose the activities. You need enough pictures to have three for each group member but having more works best.

Divide the pictures into three stacks. One stack is pictures that could represent life situations and emotions before the skillful behavior was learned. One stack represents Pass one stack to the left and the other stack to the right.

Instructions: I am going to pass around three stacks of pictures. Mindfully consider these pictures and choose one from each stack. Choose a photo that represents a skill, a photo that represents life before the skill and a photo that represents life after successfully using the skill. Be specific about the skill you choose.

Pass pictures around and have each member take three, one from each stack.

Mindfulness Readings

The Book of Awakening: Having the Life You Want by Being Present to the Life You Have. Mark Nepo

The Lorax Dr. Seuss

My Many Colored Days Seuss/Johnson & Fancher

Oh, The Places You'll Go Dr. Seuss

Peace Tales Margaret Read MacDonald

Wisdom Tales From Around the World Heather Forest

Games

Moods by Hasbro
Jenga
Bop It (Hasbro)
Bananagrams

Dance
Cha Cha Slide (2004) Download from iTunes

Movies/Television

Karate Kid (Daniel as crane is wise mind. Mr Miagi multisensory skills trainer)
Athletes (shooting from free throw line or playing golf)

Tapes/CDS

Jon Kabat- Zinn's Body Scan and Mindfulness Meditation
http://www.mindfulnesstapes.com/author.html

Made in the USA
Monee, IL
18 May 2022

96665895R00036

Mindfulness means paying attention in a particular way; on purpose, in the present moment, and nonjudgmentally. Jon Kabat-Zinn

Karyn Hall, Ph.D. is the founder and director of The Dialectical Behavior Therapy Center in Houston, Tx, and the author of The Emotionally Sensitive Person and SAVVY. She is co-author of The Power of Validation and the founder of DBTSkillsCoaching.com.

This book was made possible by the generous sharing of so many DBT therapists. Thanks to each and every person who contributed.

ISBN 9781496037381

9 781496 037381